GW01605806

SNOW WHITE AND THE SEVEN DWARFS

Retold and illustrated by
Anna and Danuta Dzierżek

PRINTED IN GREAT BRITAIN
DEAN & SON Ltd.
52 54 Southwark St. LONDON SE1 1UA
TRADE MARK

603 07761 7

Long ago, in a distant land of dark forests and high, snow-capped mountains, there was a beautiful castle. It was surrounded by lovely gardens where sweet-scented roses grew amongst beds of brightly coloured flowers and shrubs. Shady trees protected these colourful gardens from the hot sun in the summer and the cold winds in winter. There were great lawns, and ornamental pools in which gold and silver fish darted between the shimmering water-lilies.

There was one thing missing in the gardens and that was the sound of children's laughter, and this was a great disappointment to the young King and Queen who lived in the castle. They were very much in love, but also very unhappy, for they had no sons or daughters of their own.

One springtime, when the flowers were in bud, and the trees were covered in blossom, the Queen walked round the garden, sighing and looking sadly at the beauty around her. "I wish I had a daughter to share my lovely garden with," she thought.

The Queen's wish must have been heard, for on the day of the first snow a baby girl was born to her.

There should have been great rejoicing at this happy event, but alas, on the same day, the young Queen died.

The little girl was a beautiful baby. Her hair was a mass of jet black curls and her face and hands were as white as the snowflakes which fell outside the window of her nursery. Her cheeks were pink as apple blossom and her eyes as blue as the sky on a summer's day. No-one could but love her. The King decided to call his daughter Snow White.

The seasons passed in the garden. Spring was followed by summer, the leaves of the trees turned red, brown and gold in autumn, and all was white and sparkling in winter. The years came and went, and Snow White grew from a small child into a beautiful young girl. She tended the garden lovingly as her mother had done, and was loved by the birds and the other animals who lived there. She was a good daughter, and the King was sad because she did not have a mother. Eventually he decided to marry again. He had thought about this a great deal, and had met many ladies of royal blood who would make a suitable queen and mother.

His choice finally fell on a princess from a far-away country. No-one seemed to know anything of the place she came from—it was far beyond the mountains. He chose her because she was the most lovely and pleasant of all. The wedding took place amidst much rejoicing, and at last the King was happy. Snow White had a new mother.

Not long after, the King had to leave his castle to visit his cousin, the king of the neighbouring country, who was ill. He left happy in the sure knowledge that his new wife would take care of his dear Snow White.

If he had but noticed the gleam in his wife's green eyes as he bade her goodbye, he would never have gone, and this story would not have been written. But he did go, and from that day Snow White was in danger.

From her home beyond the mountains the new Queen had brought a large gold-framed mirror. This hung in her bed-chamber. But the mirror was no ordinary one, for it could speak. Each day, as the Queen combed her long hair, she would peer into it and ask:

"Mirror, mirror on the
  wall,
Who is fairest of them all?"

And each day the mirror would reply that of course the Queen was fairest. This would put her in a good temper for the rest of the morning.

One fateful day the mirror gave the wrong answer:

"Snow White is the fairest,
  that is true.
She is far lovelier than you."

The Queen was so enraged that she determined to get rid of Snow White for ever. She summoned one of her faithful servants, and told him to take Snow White into the depths of the forest and to return with only her heart, which he was to put into a small jewelled box.

The servant was not a cruel man. He did not want to kill Snow White, but he took her into the forest as the Queen had instructed him.

Once there, he told Snow White that she must never return to the castle. He left her in a small clearing and hurried away. On his way back to the castle he killed a deer and put the beast's heart into the Queen's jewelled box.

Left on her own, Snow White at first wandered happily around picking flowers and listening to the birds singing, but as the evening approached she began to get hungry and thirsty. She decided to look for a path to lead her out of the forest. This was not very easy to do. The trees cast deep shadows, and there were strange noises and rustlings all around her. She began to run.

Suddenly Snow White stopped. In front of her was a tiny gate and a path that led to the sweetest little cottage you could imagine. Snow White opened the gate and walked up to the door. No-one answered her knock, so she turned the handle. The door opened and Snow White walked in.

The inside of the cottage was very unusual, for there was only one room. There were no stairs at all. In the room stood a table with seven little chairs. Against the wall were seven little beds. There was also a large stove on which stood an array of pots and pans. The room looked rather dusty, and in the corners cobwebs hung from the ceiling.

As soon as Snow White caught sight of the beds, she wanted to go to sleep.

Of course the little beds were much too small, so she pushed them together and lay across them. She fell asleep almost immediately.

The little cottage belonged to seven little dwarfs, who worked in the nearby mountains mining precious stones and gold. As Snow White was falling asleep they were coming up the path to their home. The first dwarf opened the door and they all rushed in, stopping almost immediately in astonishment. Someone was asleep on their beds!

The bravest of the dwarfs moved forward a little to get a better look, and the others peeped out from behind him. "Oh," sighed the brave dwarf, "what a beautiful girl." The others pushed him out of the way so that they could also see. One of them bumped into a bed, and Snow White sat up in fright. "Who are you?" she cried. "I am sorry I came into your cottage."

The dwarfs quickly reassured her, and invited her to stay for as long as she wished. They even volunteered to sleep on the chairs so that she could have a comfortable night on their beds.

The next morning Snow White told them her story. The dwarfs were aghast at the wickedness of the Queen. "You must stay with us," they said. Snow White thanked them joyfully and promised to cook and keep house for them. She began straight away by dusting, and sweeping the floor.

The dwarfs went off to work happily, their minds full of their new guest.

Meanwhile, in the castle, the wicked Queen rewarded her servant for bringing Snow White's heart back from the forest. She held the box which contained the heart as she spoke to her magic mirror:

"Mirror, mirror on the wall,
Who is fairest of us all?"

The mirror replied without hesitation:

"In the forest far away
Dwells Snow White as fair as day.
Her beauty is without compare,
None in the land is half as fair."

The Queen's fury knew no bounds. She hurled the box against the wall and screamed with rage. She decided to kill Snow White herself.

She disguised herself as a gipsy woman with a basket of odds and ends to sell. Among them was a pretty, decorated comb. The comb was a special one. Before putting it into the basket the Queen dipped it in a very strong poison.

The Queen set off for the cottage. At the door she knocked and spoke in a disguised voice, "Pretty trinkets for sale, dearie. Buy a gift for your loved ones from a poor old gipsy."

Snow White had been told by the dwarfs not to open the door to strangers, so she unlatched the window and peered out. The old woman on the doorstep looked innocent enough, and the girl was curious to see what the basket contained. The old woman held the pretty comb out to her.

"See this?" she cackled. "It's the best comb in the world. It will make your pretty hair shine like a raven's wing."

Snow White could not resist this. She took the comb from the old lady and began to run it through her hair. Suddenly she fell to the floor.

The old woman laughed joyfully and hurried back to the castle to consult her mirror.

In the meantime the dwarfs returned home from work to find Snow White lying on the floor. They immediately suspected the wicked Queen of hurting her, and hurriedly removed the poisoned comb from her hair. When they had done this Snow White opened her eyes. The dwarfs made her promise never to open the door or the window to anyone again.

In the castle, the Queen was once more making evil plans, for the mirror had told her that Snow White was still alive. This time she decided to disguise herself as a farmer's wife, taking apples to market. Of course the best apple of all was full of poison.

The wicked Queen set out for the cottage of the seven dwarfs. At the door she stopped and knocked. "Who is it?" asked Snow White from the other side of the door. "I am a farmer's wife," said the Queen. "I was on my way to the market, but missed the path through the wood. I wonder if you could show me the way?"

Snow White peered out of the window. The farmer's wife looked so jolly and rosy-cheeked, and her apples shone red and green in their basket. "Surely this pleasant woman could not mean me any harm," thought Snow White. With this thought she put out of her mind all that the dwarfs had told her, and she opened the door. "Of course I will show you the way."

While Snow White was giving directions to the farmer's wife, the woman took a rosy, delicious-looking apple out of her basket and offered it to her. "Thank you for helping me," she said with a smile. "Enjoy this apple with my thanks."

Snow White took the apple and, waving goodbye to the farmer's wife, went into the cottage and shut the door. The apple was fragrant and it made her feel quite hungry. She could not resist taking a big bite.

No sooner had she done so than she fell down in a faint. The piece of apple lodged in her throat.

On their return from work the dwarfs discovered Snow White and quickly realised that her heart was no longer beating. Tearfully they sat down and thought about what they should do next, and after a while they decided to make a casket of the finest crystal. In this they would lay the body of Snow White on crimson cushions of the softest velvet. The casket would rest in her favourite leafy glade in the forest, watched over by her dearest friends.

Each day two dwarfs stood guard over the casket in which Snow White lay, looking more beautiful than ever. It is not surprising that a prince journeying through the forest felt that he must stop and admire her.

The dwarfs told him the sad story, and as they spoke the Prince raised the lid of the casket. He could not believe that Snow White was no longer alive, she was so beautiful. This sudden movement of the lid released the apple from Snow White's throat, and she sat up and blinked.

"Where am I?" she enquired. "Have I been asleep?"

The dwarfs crowded round, jumping for joy and laughing. Snow White caught sight of the Prince and a blush spread over her lovely cheeks. She smiled shyly.

The Prince helped Snow White out of the casket and lifted her onto his horse. "I shall take the Princess Snow White back with me to my father's palace," he told the dwarfs. "There she will always be safe from her wicked stepmother."

Though the dwarfs sadly bade their dear Snow White farewell, they knew that now she would be free from harm.

You can probably guess the end of this story. Snow White and the Prince fell in love and were soon married. The dwarfs were invited to the wedding and they gave Snow White a present of precious stones and gold which they had mined themselves.

As for the wicked Queen, she looked into her mirror just once more. What it told her so enraged her that she smashed it into a thousand fragments. Then she packed her belongings and set off for her own country, far beyond the mountains. If she ever got there no-one knows, for she was never seen again.